Instant jQuery Flot Visual Data Analysis

Visualize and analyze your data with the jQuery
Flot plotting library using real-world examples

Brian Peiris

PUBLISHING

BIRMINGHAM - MUMBAI

Instant jQuery Flot Visual Data Analysis

First published: October 2013

Production Reference: 1251013

Published by Packt Publishing Ltd.
Livery Place
35 Livery Street
Birmingham B3 2PB, UK.

ISBN 978-1-78328-0650

www.packtpub.com

Credits

Author

Brian Peiris

Reviewers

Alex Bliss

Marco Franssen

Mihir Mone

Acquisition Editors

Vinay Argekar

Akram Hussain

Lead Technical Editor

Manasi Pandire

Technical Editor

Novina Kewalramani

Project Coordinator

Joel Goveya

Proofreaders

Paul Hindle

Ameesha Green

Production Coordinator

Manu Joseph

Cover Work

Manu Joseph

Cover Image

Disha Haria

About the Author

Brian Peiris is a developer with a passion for the Web and all things technological. He's been programming for more than 15 years and has been a professional web developer for 7 years. Brian has followed jQuery since its inception and has used Flot extensively in commercial projects. When he's not coding, Brian enjoys tinkering with electronics, robotics, and playing the guitar and violin.

I'd like to thank my family for their support in pursuing my passion for technology, the people at Packt for the opportunity to write this book and their guidance throughout the process, and the reviewers for their time and invaluable feedback.

About the Reviewers

Alex Bliss is a software architect who enjoys planning and implementing complex software solutions to scientific and business problems, providing an effective mix of team leadership and technical knowledge. Alex enjoys implementing solutions in a wide range of fields.

Alex works for the Image Permanence Institute, maintaining their business and environmental monitoring and statistics software, as well as developing new software for various grant opportunities.

Alex has worked for over a decade in developing accessible web applications using HTML5 and JavaScript. He also has an interest in statistics and mathematical computing using Flot and jStat as well as SciPy and Matlab.

Marco Franssen is a very passionate developer from the Netherlands. During his career, he has worked on various types of software projects. These projects range from client software, distributed systems, web applications, and MS Office add-ins. Some of the techniques and languages Marco is familiar with are: C#, ASP.NET MVC, CQRS, DDD, JavaScript, NodeJS, SCRUM, Agile, and so on.

In all of these projects, Marco had a role as a lead developer or architect. Thanks to Marco's ability to think in terms of abstracts, his understanding of processes, and his analytical skills, he was able to bring all his projects success.

Marco also has a personal weblog at `http://marcofranssen.nl`, where he shares his knowledge with the community.

Currently, Marco is working as a lead developer for BlueKiwi, the European Enterprise Social Networking company. He is leading on all the third-party integrations from an architecture point of view. This will help him to make the next step in his career to eventually be promoted to architect. Marco has also given many workshops and presentations within Atos, BlueKiwi's mother company, sharing his knowledge and expertise with colleague developers, which is all over the world.

Mihir Mone is a postgraduate from Monash University, Australia. Although he completed his postgraduation in Network Computing; these days, he mainly does web and mobile development.

After spending some time fiddling around with routers and switches, he quickly decided to build on his passion for web development; not design but development. Building web systems and applications rather than websites with all the fancy flash animations was very interesting and alluring to him. He even returned to his alma mater to teach all about web development to pass forward what he had learned.

These days, he works for a small software/engineering house in Melbourne doing web development, and prototyping exciting new ideas in the data visualization and UX domain.

He is a Linux enthusiast and a big proponent of the OSS movement and believes that software should always be free to actualize its true potential. A true geek at heart, he spends some of his leisure time writing code in the hope that it may be helpful to the masses.

He is also a motorsport junkie, so you may find him loitering around race tracks from time to time (especially if there is Formula1 involved).

www.PacktPub.com

Support files, eBooks, discount offers and more

You might want to visit www.PacktPub.com for support files and downloads related to your book.

Did you know that Packt offers eBook versions of every book published, with PDF and ePub files available? You can upgrade to the eBook version at www.PacktPub.com and as a print book customer, you are entitled to a discount on the eBook copy. Get in touch with us at service@packtpub.com for more details.

At www.PacktPub.com, you can also read a collection of free technical articles, sign up for a range of free newsletters and receive exclusive discounts and offers on Packt books and eBooks.

http://PacktLib.PacktPub.com

Do you need instant solutions to your IT questions? PacktLib is Packt's online digital book library. Here, you can access, read and search across Packt's entire library of books.

Why Subscribe?

- ► Fully searchable across every book published by Packt
- ► Copy and paste, print and bookmark content
- ► On demand and accessible via web browser

Free Access for Packt account holders

If you have an account with Packt at www.PacktPub.com, you can use this to access PacktLib today and view nine entirely free books. Simply use your login credentials for immediate access.

Table of Contents

Preface

Data visualization and analysis is a key skill in today's data-driven world. Whether you need to help users understand data in your application or you're building reports to help track your business' information, you will almost certainly need the ability to create custom charts and graphs in your toolbelt.

Flot is a JavaScript and charting library based on jQuery. It allows you to create beautiful, sophisticated, and dynamic charts, graphs, and plots with ease. Flot's sensible defaults and simple API let you get started quickly.

This book guides you through Flot's features and capabilities. The recipes give you a concise introduction to Flot and its built-in plugins. You'll learn how to create various types of charts and graphs, customize the charts' options to suit your needs, and apply what you've learnt to real data.

We'll also cover some statistical methods via the jStat JavaScript library so that you can further analyze your data.

When you've mastered Flot's features, you'll learn to take advantage of its extensibility and build plugins that help you encapsulate and reuse custom functionality.

What this book covers

Creating basic charts (Must know), introduces Flot and its API. You'll learn to create the simplest types of charts and configure the charts to combine multiple series and chart types.

Creating stacked charts (Must know), covers Flot's built-in `stack` plugin, which allows you to create stacked line and bar charts. You'll also learn to use the plugin's options to group series into multiple stacks.

Creating pie charts (Must know), covers the `pie` plugin and its various options. You'll create plain pie charts, labelled charts, donut charts, tilted pie charts, and use one of the plugin's more advanced features.

Working with axes (Should know), teaches you to customize a chart's axes, transforming the shape of a graph by using a logarithmic scale, displaying multiple data series with their own independent axes, and making the axes interactive.

Tracking curves (Should know), covers the `crosshair` plugin and introduces Flot's hover event so that you can create a chart that tracks a user's mouse cursor across a graph interactively.

Plotting time series (Should know), explains the `time` plugin, which allows you to plot time-based data. You'll also learn to configure the plugin to display a custom date format.

Displaying error bars (Should know), covers the `errorbars` plugin and teaches you to display horizontal and vertical error bars on a chart.

Displaying percentiles (Should know), covers the `fillbetween` plugin, which we use to visualize percentile data.

Incorporating statistics with Flot (Should know), introduces the jStat library and uses it to calculate some basic statistical properties of data sets including standard deviation, correlation, and distribution.

Applying Flot (Should know), demonstrates how you can apply Flot to visualize real-world data. We create pie charts with data from an Open Data API and calculate averages and trends for personal weight data.

Creating custom plugins (Become an expert), introduces Flot's plugin API and teaches you to create a plugin that can add a running average to any dataset.

What you need for this book

This book uses Flot Version 0.8.1 available directly from `http://www.flotcharts.org/downloads/flot-0.8.1.zip`. You can learn more about Flot at `http://www.flotcharts.org/`.

Flot requires jQuery and works with Version 1.2.6 and above. Of course, it's best to use more recent versions of jQuery for performance and stability. jQuery 1.8.3 is included in the Flot download but you can also find it at `http://code.jquery.com/jquery/`.

Flot supports modern browsers including Firefox, Chrome, Safari, and Opera. It also supports Internet Explorer 6 and above. Internet Explorer 8 and below require an additional Explorer Canvas library, which is included in the Flot download and at `http://code.google.com/p/explorercanvas/`.

We also use the jStat library. The library does not have an official released version, but you can download the exact version used in this book from `https://github.com/jstat/jstat/archive/e4c2d0cc43c02bbfa1c99969d72659a856e2d393.zip`. Learn more about jStat at `https://github.com/jstat/jstat` and `http://jstat.github.io/`.

Who this book is for

If you're looking to add data visualization capabilities to your web application, this book is for you. You'll gain a head start that will allow you to create beautiful, powerful, and dynamic charts with ease. The book assumes that you have a working knowledge of JavaScript and jQuery.

Conventions

In this book, you will find a number of styles of text that distinguish between different kinds of information. Here are some examples of these styles, and an explanation of their meaning.

Code words in text are shown as follows: "Our HTML must include a `div` element that will contain the chart."

A block of code is set as follows:

```
<body>
  <div class="chart" id="sampleChart"></div>
  <script src="jquery.js"></script>
  <script src="jquery.flot.js"></script>
</body>
</html>
```

When we wish to draw your attention to a particular part of a code block, the relevant lines or items are set in bold:

```
<!doctype html>
<html>
<head>
  <meta charset="utf-8" />
  <title>Flot - Basic Charts</title>
  <style>
    .chart {
      width: 500px;
      height: 300px;
    }
  </style>
```

```
    </head>
    <body>
      <div class="chart" id="sampleChart"></div>
    </body>
    </html>
```

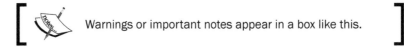

Warnings or important notes appear in a box like this.

Tips and tricks appear like this.

Reader feedback

Feedback from our readers is always welcome. Let us know what you think about this book—what you liked or may have disliked. Reader feedback is important for us to develop titles that you really get the most out of.

To send us general feedback, simply send an e-mail to feedback@packtpub.com, and mention the book title via the subject of your message.

If there is a topic that you have expertise in and you are interested in either writing or contributing to a book, see our author guide on www.packtpub.com/authors.

Customer support

Now that you are the proud owner of a Packt book, we have a number of things to help you to get the most from your purchase.

Downloading the example code

You can download the example code files for all Packt books you have purchased from your account at http://www.packtpub.com. If you purchased this book elsewhere, you can visit http://www.packtpub.com/support and register to have the files e-mailed directly to you.

Downloading the color images of this book

We also provide you a PDF file that has color images of the screenshots/diagrams used in this book. The color images will help you better understand the changes in the output. You can download this file from: http://www.packtpub.com/sites/default/files/downloads/0650OS_ColoredGraphics.pdf

Errata

Although we have taken every care to ensure the accuracy of our content, mistakes do happen. If you find a mistake in one of our books—maybe a mistake in the text or the code—we would be grateful if you would report this to us. By doing so, you can save other readers from frustration and help us improve subsequent versions of this book. If you find any errata, please report them by visiting http://www.packtpub.com/submit-errata, selecting your book, clicking on the **errata submission form** link, and entering the details of your errata. Once your errata are verified, your submission will be accepted and the errata will be uploaded on our website, or added to any list of existing errata, under the Errata section of that title. Any existing errata can be viewed by selecting your title from http://www.packtpub.com/support.

Piracy

Piracy of copyright material on the Internet is an ongoing problem across all media. At Packt, we take the protection of our copyright and licenses very seriously. If you come across any illegal copies of our works, in any form, on the Internet, please provide us with the location address or website name immediately so that we can pursue a remedy.

Please contact us at copyright@packtpub.com with a link to the suspected pirated material.

We appreciate your help in protecting our authors, and our ability to bring you valuable content.

Questions

You can contact us at questions@packtpub.com if you are having a problem with any aspect of the book, and we will do our best to address it.

Instant jQuery Flot Visual Data Analysis

Welcome to *Instant jQuery Flot – Visual Data Analysis*. Learn how to visualize data using the Flot charting library for jQuery through step-by-step recipes.

Creating basic charts (Must know)

Flot is powerful and highly configurable, but it's also easy to get started with since Flot uses sensible defaults for most of its options. This recipe will teach you how to create the simplest types of charts.

You can download Flot from `http://www.flotcharts.org/`. Refer to the *What you need for this book* section for more information about Flot and jQuery versions and supported browsers.

Getting ready

Flot requires a few lines of HTML and CSS boilerplate to begin with. Our HTML must include a `div` element that will contain the chart. The `div` element must have a width and height defined; we do that with some CSS as follows:

```
<!doctype html>
<html>
<head>
  <meta charset="utf-8" />
  <title>Flot - Basic Charts</title>
  <style>
```

```
    .chart {
      width: 500px;
      height: 300px;
    }
  </style>
</head>
<body>
  <div class="chart" id="sampleChart"></div>
</body>
</html>
```

Since Flot is a jQuery plugin, we must, of course, include jQuery before we include Flot itself as follows:

```
...
<body>
  <div class="chart" id="sampleChart"></div>
  <script src="jquery.js"></script>
  <script src="jquery.flot.js"></script>
</body>
</html>
```

How to do it...

Once we have the boilerplate code in place, we can start creating charts. We'll start with simple line charts, point charts, bar charts, and area charts.

Line charts

We can create the simplest line chart with just a few lines of JavaScript code:

```
...
<body>
  <div class="chart" id="sampleChart"></div>
  <script src="jquery.js"></script>
```

```
<script src="jquery.flot.js"></script>
<script>
  $('#sampleChart').plot(
      [ [[0, 3], [1, -1], [2, 2]] ],
      { series: { lines: {show: true} } }
  );
</script>
</body>
</html>
```

This creates a chart with a line ranging from 0 to 2 on the X axis and -1 to 3 on the Y axis. Flot draws the grid and tick labels for us automatically:

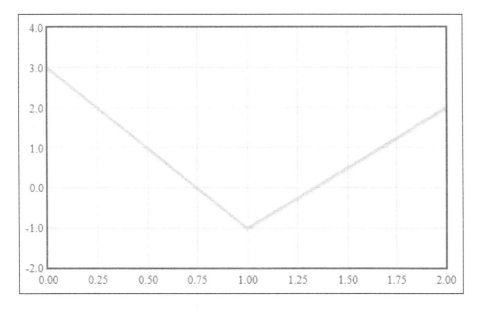

Point charts

Creating bar charts and point charts is just as easy. Simply change the chart option from `lines` to `points` in order to create a point chart as follows:

```
...
<script>
  $('#sampleChart').plot(
      [ [[0, 3], [1, -1], [2, 2]] ],
      { series: { points: {show: true} } }
  );
</script>
...
```

Bar charts

Change the option to `bars` in order to create a bar chart, as shown in the following code:

```
...
<script>
  $('#sampleChart').plot(
    [ [[0, 3], [1, -1], [2, 2]] ],
    { series: { bars: {show: true} } }
  );
</script>
...
```

Once again, Flot draws a bar chart with the range of values, grid and tick labels, as expected. A colored bar is drawn for each data point:

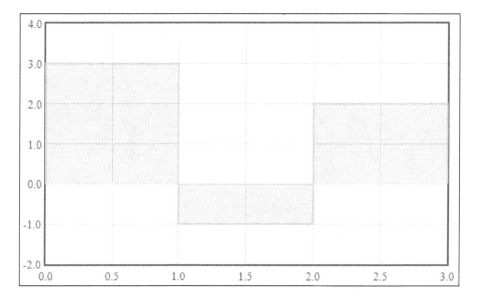

Area charts

An area chart is just a line chart with the `fill` option specified, as shown in the following code:

```
...
<script>
  $('#sampleChart').plot(
    [ [[0, 3], [1, -1], [2, 2]] ],
    { series: { lines: {show: true, fill: true} } }
  );
</script>
...
```

Flot fills in the region between the data point and a horizontal line at the origin:

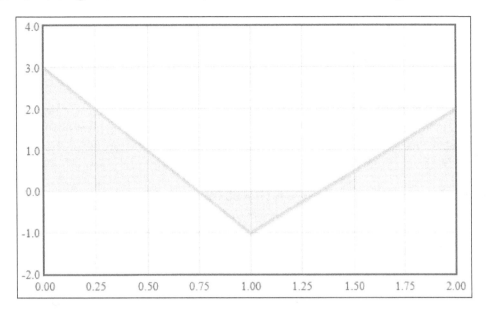

How it works...

We first started by defining a `div` element in our HTML as a placeholder for our chart. Flot uses this element as a container. You can see this in action by using Firebug or your browser's equivalent development tool to inspect the contents of the element after Flot has drawn the chart. Flot creates multiple `canvas` elements as well as some other `div` elements in order to construct the chart that we specify.

Since the chart is often part of a larger set of HTML content, Flot does not assume anything about the size of the chart. Instead, we must specify our intended size by setting the CSS properties of the container element.

Lastly, we invoke Flot by calling the `plot` function via the jQuery object, passing in our container element, our chart data, and our chart options:

```
$(<placeholder>).plot(<data>, <options>);
```

The chart data is represented as a set of nested arrays. The first level is an array of series, which is a group of data. The second level is a data set, which is a set of data points. The last level is a data point; an x and y coordinate as shown in the following code:

```
[ [ [0, 1], [1, 2] ] ]
Data: [ series1, series2 ]
Series: [ datapoint1, datapoint2 ]
Datapoint: [ x1, y1 ]
```

We use the `options` object to specify which type of chart should be used to display our data. The object has a `series` property whose value determines the options applied to all series. We set the `show` property of the `lines`, `points`, or `bars` objects to enable that particular chart type.

There's more...

Flot's sensible default options give you a good starting point without too much effort. However, there are many more configurations and options available to us. You can learn about all the options (including the `grid` and `legend` configuration options, which we don't cover in this book) at `https://github.com/flot/flot/blob/0.8.1/API.md`.

Displaying multiple series on the same chart

The preceding examples use only one series in the data. We can add more series to our data options and Flot will display them accordingly. The options specified in the `series` object are applied to all series:

```
. . .
<script>
  $('#sampleChart').plot(
    [
      [[0, 3], [1, -1], [2, 2]],
      [[0, 1], [1, 3], [2, -2]]
    ],
    { series: { lines: {show: true} } }
  );
</script>
. . .
```

Flot draws a single chart with the series overlapping each other in same order as the data array:

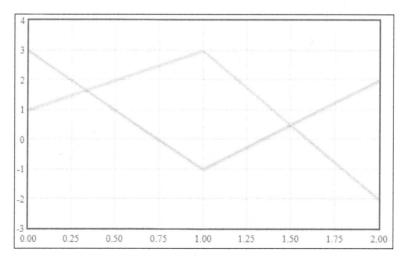

Using different chart types for each series

Flot allows us to specify different options for each series by using a different data options format. Instead of directly specifying a data set for each series, we specify a `series` object. The `series` object contains a data set and can contain options that apply to that series alone. In this case, we show one data set using the `lines` chart type and the other using the `bars` chart type. The bars in the bar chart are aligned to the center of the data point via the `align` option, as shown in the following code:

```
...
   <script>
     $('#sampleChart').plot(
       [
         {
           data: [[0, 3], [1, -1], [2, 2]],
           lines: {show: true}
         },
         {
           data: [[0, 1], [1, 3], [2, -2]],
           bars: {show: true, align: 'center'}
         }
       ]
     );
   </script>
...
```

Once again, Flot will draw a single chart with the bar chart series overlapping the line series:

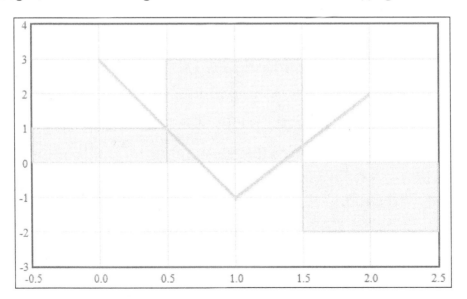

Creating stacked charts (Must know)

Flot includes a plugin that allows you to create stacked charts. Stacked charts are especially useful when the data in your series is meant to add up to some total value, for example percentage data.

Getting ready

Using the same boilerplate that we wrote in the *Creating basic charts* recipe, we just need to include the `stack` plugin, as shown in the following code:

```
. . .
<script src="jquery.js"></script>
<script src="jquery.flot.js"></script>
<script src="jquery.flot.stack.js"></script>
. . .
```

How to do it...

Using the `stack` plugin is simply a matter of specifying the `stack` option. Stacked charts work best with bar charts and area charts.

Stacked bar charts

```
. . .
<script src="jquery.flot.stack.js"></script>
<script>
  $('#sampleChart').plot(
    [
      { color: 'orange',
        data: [[0, 3], [1, 4], [2, 2]] },
      { color: 'lightblue',
        data: [[0, 6], [1, 3], [2, 6]] },
      { color: 'darkred',
        data: [[0, 1], [1, 3], [2, 2]] }
    ],
    {
      series: {
        stack: true,
```

```
            bars: {
              show: true,
              barWidth: 0.2, align: 'center'
            }
          }
        }
      );
    </script>
    . . .
```

The `stack` plugin will draw a chart that stacks the first points of each series together into one composite bar and the second points of each series into another bar, and so on:

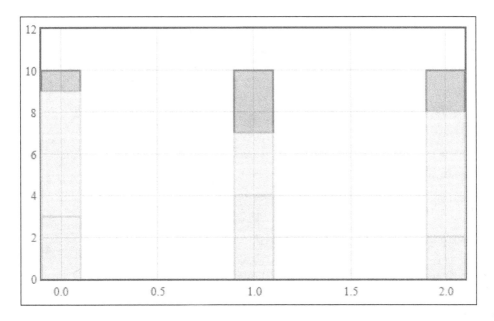

Stacked area charts

Stacked area charts are simply stack line charts with the `fill` option set to `true`:

```
. . .
    {
      series: {
        stack: true,
        lines: { show: true, fill: true }
      }
    }
. . .
```

The `stack` plugin will draw an area chart with each filled area stacked on top of each other:

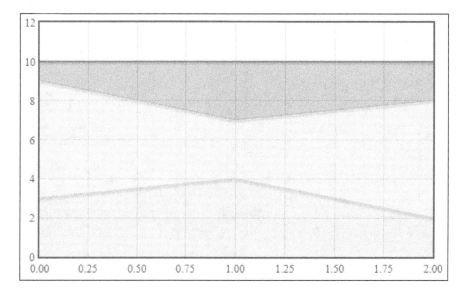

How it works...

The `stack` plugin takes the data you specify and readjusts it in such a way that the corresponding data points in the series are offset from each other. The `stack` plugin assumes that the series are already ordered from bottom to top. In this case, the first series is yellow in the chart, the second is blue, and the last is red.

There's more...

The `stack` plugin is quite simple. It only has one option, stack, but it can be used in an alternate way to create multiple groups of stacks on the same chart.

Grouping series in to multiple stacks

The `stack` plugin also has the ability to group series to separate stacks. This is done by specifying a unique key on the `stack` option of each series. The key can be any unique number or string. We combine this option with Flot's `align` option on bar charts in order to display the stacks side-by-side:

```
. . .
    $('#sampleChart').plot(
      [
        { color: 'orange',
          data: [[0, 1], [1, 5], [2, 2]],
          stack: 0, bars: {align: 'left'} },
        { color: 'lightblue',
          data: [[0, 9], [1, 5], [2, 8]],
          stack: 0, bars: {align: 'left'} },
        { color: 'darkred',
          data: [[0, 3], [1, 8], [2, 6]],
          stack: 1, bars: {align: 'right'} },
        { color: 'green',
          data: [[0, 7], [1, 2], [2, 4]],
          stack: 1, bars: {align: 'right'} }
      ],
      {
        series: {
          bars: { show: true, barWidth: 0.2 }
        }
      }
    );
. . .
```

The `stack` plugin now draws a chart where the light blue and orange series are grouped into stack `0` and the green and dark red series are grouped into stack `1`:

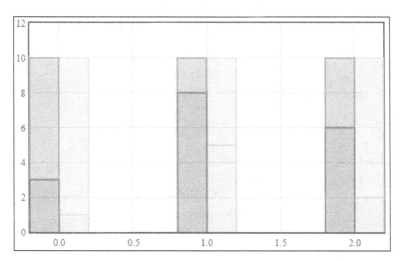

Creating pie charts (Must know)

Similar to the `stack` plugin, Flot also includes a plugin that adds pie chart capabilities.

Getting ready

Include the following `pie` plugin:

```
. . .
<script src="jquery.js"></script>
<script src="jquery.flot.js"></script>
<script src="jquery.flot.pie.js"></script>
. . .
```

How to do it...

The pie plugin uses sensible defaults for all of its options, just like Flot. We simply need to enable the plugin in order to create a simple pie chart and a labelled pie chart.

A simple pie chart

The `pie` plugin expects multiple series. It takes the first y coordinate in each series and uses it to draw the pie section for that series, as shown in the following code:

```
. . .
<script src="jquery.flot.pie.js"></script>
<script>
  $('#sampleChart').plot(
    [
      [[0, 1]],
      [[0, 2]]
    ],
    {
      series: {
        pie: { show: true }
      }
    }
  );
</script>
. . .
```

The `pie` plugin draws a bare pie chart based on our data:

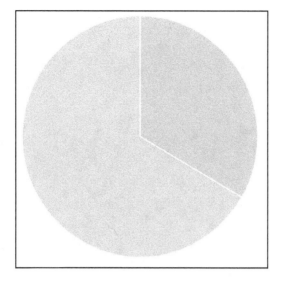

A labeled pie chart

The `pie` plugin also supports a secondary format that allows you to specify a label corresponding to each pie section. The labels are displayed in a legend as follows:

```
...
<script src="jquery.flot.pie.js"></script>
<script>
  $('#sampleChart').plot(
    [
      {label: 'Series 1', data: 10},
      {label: 'Series 2', data: 60}
    ],
    {
      series: {
        pie: { show: true }
      }
    }
  );
</script>
...
```

The legend is drawn to the right of the pie chart with the names and corresponding colors of the series:

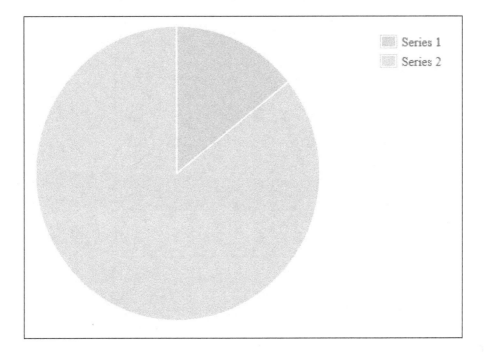

How it works...

Like the `stack` plugin, enabling the `pie` plugin is simply a matter of setting the `show` property of the `pie` settings object to `true`. However, the `pie` plugin will not accept the typical data format we've used so far. Since each series is represented by one section of the pie, the chart data can only have one data point per series.

The sum of the data points represents the whole of the pie chart. So, datapoint `[0, 1]` and datapoint `[0, 2]` represent one third of the pie and two thirds of the pie, respectively.

There's more...

The `pie` plugin includes many settings that determine how the pie chart is displayed. The settings affect the size of the pie, its shape, its rendering style including its border and shadow style, the format and styles for labels, and the behavior of "combined" sections of the pie. All of these settings are described in full on the documentation page at `http://www.flotcharts.org/flot/examples/series-pie/index.html`. Refer to the following sections for some examples of these settings.

Creating a tilted donut chart

The `pie` plugin includes settings that allow you to display donut charts. It also has an option that tilts the chart to give it a pseudo-3D effect. We specify an inner radius that turns the chart into a donut chart and a tilt setting as well. The radius setting ensures that the pie chart is small enough for Flot to draw the shadow underneath it as follows:

```
. . .
<script src="jquery.flot.pie.js"></script>
<script>
  $('#sampleChart').plot(
    [
      [[0, 1]],
      [[0, 2]]
    ],
    {
      series: {
        pie: {
          show: true,
          radius: 0.8,
          innerRadius: 0.6,
          tilt: 0.3
        }
      }
    }
  );
</script>
. . .
```

The pie plugin mimics a 3D donut effect by drawing an elliptical pie chart with a white ellipse in the center:

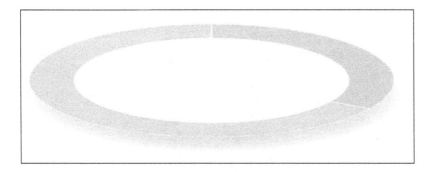

Creating a labeled pie chart with combined sections

Here we turn the `legend` setting off, which causes the `pie` plugin to render labels near the `pie` sections, and we also use the `combine` and `threshold` settings to combine the two smallest sections into one. In this case, we specify a threshold of `0.10`, which means that any series that has a value less than 10 percent of the sum of all the series is combined into a single section of the pie labeled `Other` as follows:

```
. . .
$('#sampleChart').plot(
  [
    {label: 'Series 1', data: 1},
    {label: 'Series 2', data: 2},
    {label: 'Series 3', data: 10},
    {label: 'Series 4', data: 60},
  ],
  {
    legend: { show: false },
    series: {
      pie: {
        show: true,
        combine: {
          threshold: 0.10
        }
      }
    }
  }
);
. . .
```

This results in a simplified pie chart that eliminates clutter from the visualization:

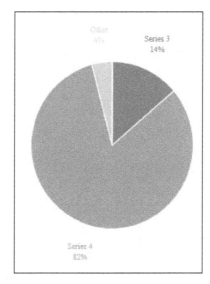

Working with axes (Should know)

The axes are the most configurable parts of the chart. Flot gives you the ability to change the position, type, and colors of the axes. It also gives you full control of the ticks and labels on the axes, letting you adjust the number of ticks and alter the formatting. Axes also determine how the data is displayed; you can change the `min` and `max` settings to display only a part of the data on the chart and you can also transform the data in various ways.

The full documentation is available at `https://github.com/flot/flot/blob/master/API.md#customizing-the-axes`. We will take a look at some examples of the configuration options by creating a chart that has a logarithmic axis and another chart that includes multiple axes.

Getting ready

We start with the same boilerplate that we used when creating basic charts.

How to do it...

The following code creates some sample data that grows exponentially. We then use the `transform` and `tickSize` setting on the Y axis to adjust how our data is displayed:

```
...
<script>
  var data = [], i;
  for (i = 1; i <= 50; i++) {
    data.push([i, Math.exp(i / 10, 2)]);
  }

  $('#sampleChart').plot(
    [ data ],
    {
      yaxis: {
        transform: function (v) {
          return v == 0 ? v : Math.log(v);
        },
        tickSize: 50
      }
    }
```

```
        );
    </script>
...
```

Flot draws a chart with a logarithmic Y axis, so that our exponential data is easier to read:

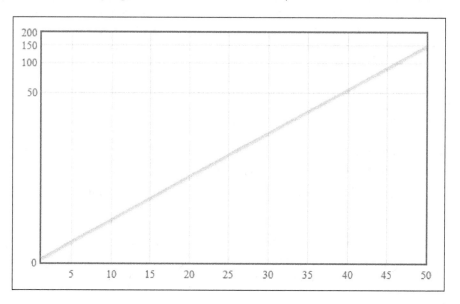

Next, we use Flot's ability to display multiple axes on the same chart as follows:

```
...
var sine = [];
for (i = 0; i < Math.PI * 2; i += 0.1) {
  sine.push([i, Math.sin(i)]);
}
var cosine = [];
for (i = 0; i < Math.PI * 2; i += 0.1) {
  cosine.push([i, Math.cos(i) * 20]);
}
$('#sampleChart').plot(
  [
    {label: 'sine', data: sine},
    {
      label: 'cosine',
      data: cosine,
      yaxis: 2
    }
  ],
```

```
        { yaxes: [ {}, { position: 'right' } ] }
    );
...
```

Flot draws the two series overlapping each other. The Y axis for the sine series is drawn on the left by default and the Y axis for the cosine series is drawn on the right as specified:

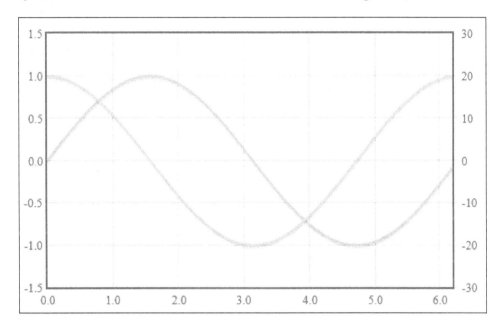

<h1>How it works...</h1>

The transform setting expects a function that takes a value, which is the y coordinate of our data, and returns a transformed value. In this case, we calculate the logarithm of our original data value so that our exponential data is displayed on a linear scale. We also use the tickSize setting to ensure that our labels do not overlap after the axis has been transformed.

The yaxis setting under the series object is a number that specifies which axis the series should be associated with. When we specify the number 2, Flot automatically draws a second axis on the chart. We then use the yaxes setting to specify that the second axis should be positioned on the right of the chart.

In this case, the sine data ranges from **-1.0** to **1.0**, whereas the cosine data ranges from **-20** to **20**. The cosine axis is drawn on the right and is independent of the sine axis.

There's more...

Flot doesn't have a built-in ability to interact with axes, but it does give you all the information you need to construct a solution.

Making axes interactive

Here, we use Flot's `getAxes` method to add interactivity to our axes as follows:

```
...
var
  showFahrenheit = false,

  temperatureFormatter = function (val, axis) {
    if (showFahrenheit) {
      val = val * 9 / 5 + 32;
    }
    return val.toFixed(1);
  },

  drawPlot = function () {
    var plot = $.plot(
      '#sampleChart',
      [[[0, 0], [1, 3], [3, 1]]],
      { yaxis: { tickFormatter: temperatureFormatter } }
    );

    var plotPlaceholder = plot.getPlaceholder();

    $.each(plot.getAxes(), function (i, axis) {
      var box = axis.box;
      var axisTarget = $('<div />');

      axisTarget.
        css({
          position: 'absolute',
          left: box.left,
          top: box.top,
          width: box.width,
          height: box.height
        }).
```

```
        click(function () {
          showFahrenheit = !showFahrenheit;
          drawPlot();
        }).
        appendTo(plotPlaceholder);
    });
  };

  drawPlot();
  . . .
```

First, note that we use a different way of creating a plot. Instead of calling the `plot` method on a jQuery collection that matches the placeholder element, we use the `plot` method directly from the jQuery object. This gives us immediate access to the Flot object, which we use to get the axes of our chart. You could have also used the following data method to gain access to the Flot object:

```
var plot = $('#sampleChart').plot(...).data('plot');
```

Once we have the Flot object, we use the `getAxes` method to retrieve a list of axis objects. We use jQuery's `each` method to iterate over each axis and we create a `div` element that acts as a target for interaction. We set the `div` element's CSS so that it is in the same position and size as the axis' bounding box, and we attach an event handler to the `click` event before appending the `div` element to the plot's placeholder element.

In this case, the event handler toggles a Boolean flag and redraws the plot. The flag determines whether the axis labels are displayed in Fahrenheit or Celsius, by changing the result of the function specified in the `tickFormatter` setting.

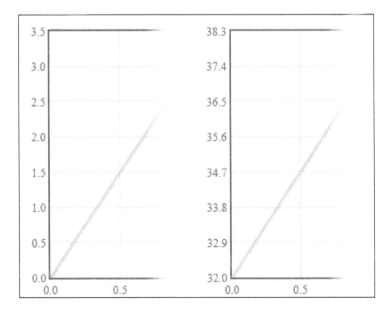

Tracking curves (Should know)

Another of Flot's built-in plugins, the `crosshair` plugin, allows you to draw a crosshair on top of a chart as the mouse moves over it. We will use this in conjunction with Flot's hover event to track the coordinates that lie under the mouse.

Getting ready

Again, we will use the same boilerplate code that we introduced while creating basic charts. We must also include the `crosshair` plugin as follows:

```
. . .
<script src="jquery.js"></script>
<script src="jquery.flot.js"></script>
<script src="jquery.flot.crosshair.js"></script>
. . .
```

How to do it...

The simplest use of the plugin displays a crosshair at the mouse position:

```
. . .
var data = [[0, 1], [1, 3], [2, 2]];
$('#sampleChart').plot(
  [ data ],
  { crosshair: { mode: 'xy' } }
);
. . .
```

The crosshairs are drawn dynamically underneath the mouse as it moves across the chart:

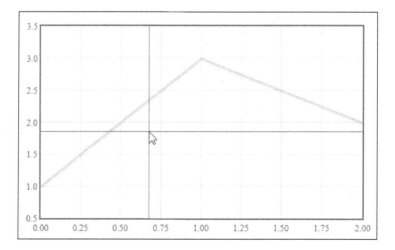

We can also use Flot's hover event to display the coordinates of the mouse position:

```
. . .
<div class="chart" id="sampleChart"></div>
<span id="coords"></span>
<script src="jquery.js"></script>
<script src="jquery.flot.js"></script>
<script src="jquery.flot.crosshair.js"></script>
<script>
  var data = [[0, 1], [1, 3], [2, 2]];

  var plot = $.plot(
    '#sampleChart',
    [ data ],
    { grid: { hoverable: true } }
  );
  plot.getPlaceholder().on(
    'plothover',
    function (event, pos) {
      $('#coords').text(
        pos.x.toFixed(2) + ', ' +
        pos.y.toFixed(2)
      );
    }
  );
. . .
```

The label below the graph dynamically displays the coordinates, in chart units, of the point under the mouse:

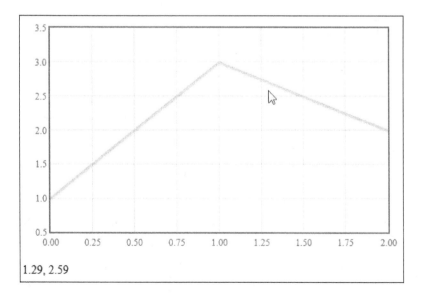

The `crosshair` plugin is very straightforward. Its settings include color and style configuration as well as a `mode` setting that can be set to x, y, or xy, depending on which axis of the crosshair you wish to display. The plugin also includes methods that allow you to set, lock, and clear the crosshair, as we'll see later.

The hover event occurs on the plot's placeholder element. The event arguments include the standard jQuery event object and a `pos` object that holds the x and y coordinates of the mouse cursor. In order to use the hover event, we must set the `hoverable` setting on the `grid` object to `true`.

These techniques allow us to construct a visual aid that helps users pinpoint the values of a series:

Tracking a curve with the crosshair

We can combine Flot's hover event with the crosshair to display a crosshair on the curve produced from our data. The crosshair will follow the horizontal position of the mouse and will always lie on the curve:

```
. . .
var plot = $.plot(
  '#sampleChart',
  [ data ],
  { grid: { hoverable: true }, crosshair: {mode: 'xy'} }
);
plot.getPlaceholder().on(
  'plothover',
  function (event, pos) {
    var j;
    for (j = 0; j < data.length; j++) {
      if (data[j][0] > pos.x) {
        break;
      }
    }

    var
      y,
      p1 = data[j - 1],
      p2 = data[j];
```

```
if (p1 == null) {
  y = p2[1];
} else if (p2 == null) {
  y = p1[1];
} else {
  y = (
    p1[1] + (p2[1] - p1[1]) *
    (pos.x - p1[0]) / (p2[0] - p1[0])
  );
}

plot.lockCrosshair({x: pos.x, y: y});
}
);
```

. . .

In our hover event handler, we use the x coordinate of the mouse to get the closest data point in our dataset. If that point is in the middle of the dataset, we try to interpolate the y coordinate by calculating the midpoint between the point and the previous point. Finally, we use the `lockCrosshair` method to display the crosshair on the curve.

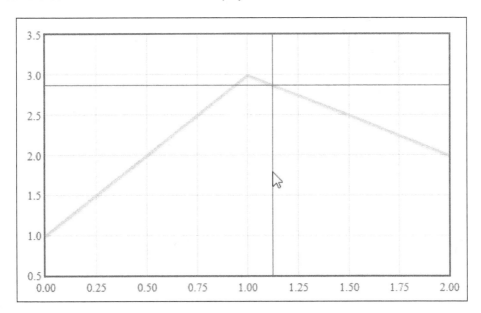

Plotting time series

Flot includes a plugin that handles time-based data. The plugin takes care of displaying the X axis accordingly, including date formatting, time zone calculations, and unit conversions.

Getting ready

Again, we can use the same boilerplate along with the `time` plugin:

```
. . .
    <script src="jquery.js"></script>
    <script src="jquery.flot.js"></script>
    <script src="jquery.flot.time.js"></script>
. . .
```

How to do it...

We enable the `time` plugin by setting `mode` to `time` on the `xaxis` setting. The `time` plugin also expects a specific data type for the x coordinates of our dataset as follows:

```
. . .
    var data = [
        [1357016400000, 0],
        [1359694800000, 4],
        [1362114000000, 2]
    ];

    $('#sampleChart').plot(
        [ data ],
        { xaxis: { mode: 'time' } }
    );
. . .
```

The time plugin automatically draws the points in their appropriate positions on the chart and also changes the labels on the X axis to display the corresponding dates:

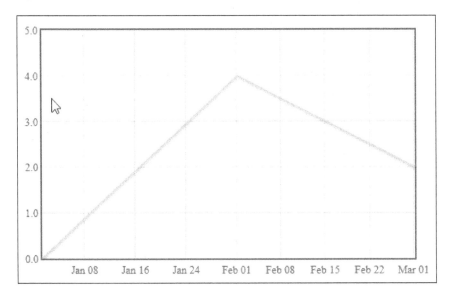

How it works...

The `time` plugin expects the x coordinates of our data set to be standard JavaScript timestamps. They represent the number of milliseconds since January 1, 1970 00:00:00 UTC. You can obtain these timestamps in JavaScript by using the `getTime` method on a `Date` object.

The plugin also assumes that the timestamps are in the UTC time zone. You may set the `timezone` setting under the `xaxis` setting to browser, if your data is in the user's time zone already. Other time zones are supported through a third-party `timezoneJS` plugin that you can find at `https://github.com/mde/timezone-js`.

The `time` plugin also includes settings to control the number of ticks displayed on the axis to use a twelve hour clock format and to change the text displayed for months and days. You can find more information in the Flot documentation available at `https://github.com/flot/flot/blob/0.8.1/API.md#time-series-data`.

There's more...

The `time` plugin also supports custom date and time formats using a formatting string that is a subset of the `strftime` standard from the C programming language. You can find more details in the preceding linked documentation.

Using custom date and time formats

Here we use a custom formatting string to force the `time` plugin to show the full date and time on the X axis labels as follows:

```
. . .
var data = [
    [new Date('2013-02-28T22:30:00Z').getTime(), 0],
    [new Date('2013-02-28T23:45:00Z').getTime(), 4],
    [new Date('2013-03-01T01:15:00Z').getTime(), 2]
];

$('#sampleChart').plot(
    [ data ],
    { xaxis: {
      mode: 'time',
      timeformat: '%Y-%m-%d %H:%M'
    } }
);
. . .
```

The labels on the X axis are replaced with text in the format we've specified:

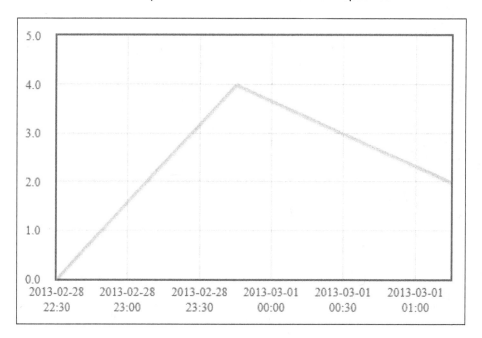

Displaying error bars (Should know)

Now that we've learned how to create various types of charts, we can start applying Flot to our real-world data. Statistical data is often accompanied by error margins and visualized on charts using error bars. Flot's `errorbars` plugin is built specifically for that scenario.

Getting ready

We start with the same boilerplate code that we used to create basic charts and we include the `errorbars` plugin.

How to do it...

The error bars are displayed with a combination of extra data values, the `errorbars` and `yerr` settings, and other settings which help produce a properly formatted chart:

```
. . .
<script src="jquery.flot.errorbars.js"></script>
<script>
  var data = [
    [1, 2, 0.5],
    [2, 5, 0.2],
    [3, 1, 0.4]
  ];

  var plot = $.plot(
    $('.chart'),
    [ data ],
    {
      series: {
        lines: { show: true },
        points: {
          show: true,
          errorbars: 'y',
          yerr: {
            show: true,
            color: 'red',
            upperCap: '-',
            lowerCap: '-'
          }
        }
```

```
        },
        xaxis: { min: 0, max: 4 },
    }
  );
</script>
...
```

Error bars are drawn in red with short horizontal lines as end caps, as specified:

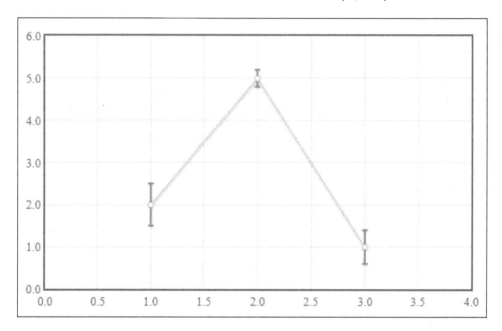

How it works...

The `errorbars` plugin expects us to provide extra data values that specify the margin of error for each data point. The margin of error is in the same unit as the y value of the data point. In the preceding example, we've specified the values `0.5`, `0.2`, and `0.4` respectively.

We enable the `errorbars` plugin by setting the `errorbars` setting to `y`. This tells the plugin to use the extra data value as an error bar on the Y axis. The `yerr` settings object allows us to specify how the error bars should be displayed. We set the `color`, `upperCap`, and `lowerCap` settings so that the error bars are more easily visible.

We also enable the `show` settings on the `lines` and `points` setting objects so that both lines and points are drawn on the graph. Finally, we explicitly set the `min` and `max` settings on the `xaxis` settings object so that our data points are easier to see on the chart.

There's more...

The `errorbars` plugin has the ability to display error bars on the X axis as well. It also gives you the ability to display asymmetric errors and custom end-cap styles.

Using custom end caps on an asymmetric, horizontal error bar

Here, we use a combination of the `asymmetric` setting and custom functions for the `upperCap` and `lowerCap` settings to display a square end cap. The `squareCap` function receives a canvas context object (the DOM CanvasRenderingContext2D type) which we use to draw a square at the given X and Y coordinates:

```
...
data = [
  [1, 2, 0.1, 0.4],
  [2, 5, 0.5, 0.2],
  [3, 1, 0.1, 0.2]
];

var squareCap = function (ctx, x, y, radius) {
  ctx.beginPath();
  var r2 = radius / 2;
  ctx.rect(x - r2, y - r2, radius, radius);
  ctx.stroke();
};

var plot = $.plot(
  $('.chart'),
  [ data ],
  {
    series: {
      lines: { show: true },
      points: {
        show: true,
        errorbars: 'x',
        xerr: {
          show: true,
          asymmetric: true,
          color: 'red',
          upperCap: squareCap,
          lowerCap: squareCap,
          radius: 10
```

```
                }
              }
            },
            xaxis: { min: 0, max: 4 },
        }
      );
  . . .
```

Asymettric error bars expect two error values in the data points. The error bars are drawn independently to the left and right of the data points. Our square caps are rendered as empty red boxes on the ends of the bars:

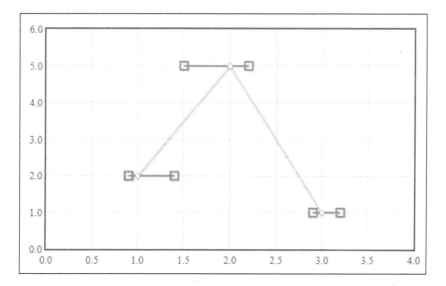

Displaying percentiles (Should know)

Flot's `fillbetween` plugin allows you to visualize percentiles by shading the area between the series that represent each percentile.

Getting ready

Include the `fillbetween` plugin as follows:

```
  . . .
    <script src="jquery.js"></script>
    <script src="jquery.flot.js"></script>
    <script src="jquery.flot.fillbetween.js"></script>
  . . .
```

How to do it...

The plugin uses `id` and `fillBetween` settings on each series object to identify and configure the filled areas:

```
...
<script src="jquery.flot.fillbetween.js"></script>
<script>
  var data = {
    '25%': [
      [0, 53], [1, 56], [2, 60], [3, 60], [4, 66],
      [5, 72], [6, 71], [7, 74], [8, 76], [9, 80]
    ],
    '50%': [
      [0, 69], [1, 67], [2, 74], [3, 71], [4, 76],
      [5, 79], [6, 77], [7, 81], [8, 82], [9, 85]
    ],
    '75%': [
      [0, 83], [1, 84], [2, 89], [3, 84], [4, 85],
      [5, 86], [6, 86], [7, 88], [8, 91], [9, 93]
    ],
    '90%': [
      [0, 90], [1, 92], [2, 93], [3, 92], [4, 92],
      [5, 93], [6, 91], [7, 93], [8, 94], [9, 95]
    ],
    'mean': [
      [0, 68.44], [1, 70.19], [2, 73.71], [3, 71.97],
      [4, 75.98], [5, 78.86], [6, 78.86], [7, 81.33],
      [8, 83.35], [9, 85.82]
    ]
  };
  var dataset = [
    { id: '25%', data: data['25%'], lines:{ fill: false } },
    { id: '50%', data: data['50%'], fillBetween: '25%' },
    { id: '75%', data: data['75%'], fillBetween: '50%' },
    { id: '90%', data: data['90%'], fillBetween: '75%' },
    { id: 'mean', data: data['mean'], lines:{ fill: false} }
  ];

  $.plot(
    $('.chart'),
    dataset,
    {
```

```
            lines: { fill: 0.5 },
            shadowSize: 0
        }
    );
    </script>
    . . .
```

The plugin draws filled regions that help visualize the volume of the space between series:

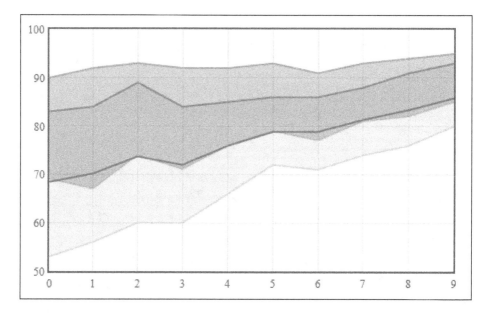

How it works...

The `fillbetween` plugin is similar to the `stack` plugin. It takes your data and manipulates it so that the area between the specified series are filled, or shaded. The plugin does not calculate percentiles for you—it can be applied to any series—but it is especially useful for visualizing percentile data.

The plugin requires that you identify each series with the `id` setting so that you can refer to them in the `fillBetween` setting. In this case, we identify our series with names as `25%`, `50%`, and so on. We then fill the area between the appropriate series by using the `fillBetween` setting. For example, we shade the area between the `50%` series and the `25%` series by setting the `fillBetween` setting on the `50%` series to `25%`.

Incorporating statistics with Flot (Should know)

Although Flot provides everything you need for visualization, it doesn't include the typical statistical calculations you might want to perform on your raw data. Here, we will learn how to use the jStat library to process your raw data so that it can be visualized with Flot.

jStat includes a large range of advanced statistical calculations. You can view its documentation online at `http://jstat.github.io/index.html`.

Getting ready

You can download jStat from its GitHub repository at `https://github.com/jstat/jstat`. We will be using some of the calculations in its `vector` and `linearalgebra` modules:

```
. . .
  <script src="jquery.js"></script>
  <script src="jquery.flot.js"></script>
  <script src="jstat/core.js"></script>
  <script src="jstat/linearalgebra.js"></script>
  <script src="jstat/vector.js"></script>
. . .
```

How to do it...

We use jStat's functions to analyze our data in various ways as follows:

```
. . .
    var yvalues = [3, 5, 2, 3, 6, 9, 3, 8, 7, 1];
    var n = yvalues.length;

    var mean = jStat.mean(yvalues);
    var median = jStat.median(yvalues);
    var mode = jStat.mode(yvalues);
    var stdev = jStat.stdev(yvalues);

    var xvalues = jStat(0, n - 1, n);
    var data = jStat([xvalues[0], yvalues]).transpose();
    var corrcoeff = jStat.corrcoeff(yvalues, xvalues[0]);

    var display = function (label, value) {
      $('#sample').
```

```
              before(label + ': ' + value.toFixed(3) + '<br />');
        };
        display('Standard deviation', stdev);
        display('Correlation coefficient', corrcoeff);

        var line = function (y) {
          return [ [0, y], [n - 1, y] ];
        };

        $.plot(
          $('#sample'),
          [
            { data: data, points: {show: true}, color: 'black' },
            { label: 'mean', data: line(mean) },
            { label: 'median', data: line(median) },
            { label: 'mode', data: line(mode) }
          ],
          { legend: { position: 'nw' } }
        );
      </script>
...
```

The data is displayed along with multiple types of analysis information:

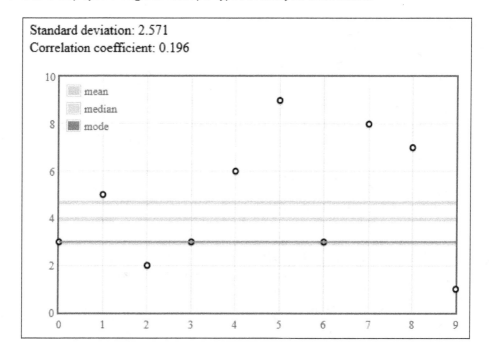

How it works...

jStat, like most statistical and mathematical software, operates on vectors and matrices. So, we represent our data, `yvalues`, as a vector in the form of an array of y values. We then use jStat to calculate the **mean, median, mode**, and **standard deviation (stdev)** of those y values.

The main `jStat` function can be used to produce a sequence of values. We use this to create `xvalues`, an array that contains a sequence from 0 to 9 (`[0, 1, 2, ..., 9]`). The `jStat` function can also be used to create a matrix. We do this with our `xvalues` and `yvalues` vectors and use the `transpose` function to create a matrix which happens to be in the same structure that Flot can plot, that is `transpose` takes a matrix like the following matrix:

- `[ [0, 1, 2], [7, 8, 9] ]`

It produces a matrix like the following matrix:

- `[ [0, 7], [1, 8], [2, 9] ]`

Next, we use jStat's `corrcoeff` function to calculate the correlation coefficient between our data and `xvalues`.

Finally, we display all of this information. We display the standard deviation and correlation as text, and we use Flot to plot the data points as well as three horizontal lines that represent the mean, median, and mode.

There's more...

jStat also comes with a large variety of probability distribution calculations, which are typical tools in statistical analysis. These include the normal (Gaussian) distribution, Beta distribution, Chi-squared distribution, Poisson distribution, and much more.

Plotting a normal distribution curve

You can calculate the data points for a normal distribution curve in only a few lines. Simply input your mean and standard deviation values into the `normal` function and use the `pdf` function to retrieve the y values:

```
...
var numPoints = 50;

var mean = 10;
var stdev = 5;
var span = stdev * 4;

var xvalues = jStat(mean - span, mean + span, numPoints + 1);
```

```
var normalDistribution = xvalues.normal(mean, stdev).pdf();

var normalPlot = jStat([
  xvalues[0],
  normalDistribution[0]
]).transpose();

$.plot( $('.chart'), [ normalPlot ] );
...
```

Flot draws the distribution curve centered at our mean value:

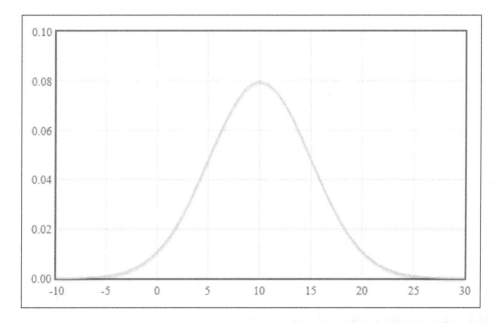

Applying Flot (Should know)

Now that we've learned how Flot works, we can apply it to our own data sources. Since we can't cover all possible uses of Flot's capabilities, we'll try to demonstrate some examples of how Flot can be applied to real-world data.

There are a myriad of data sources out there and many of them offer their data freely as Open Data sources. One of those sources is The World Bank. They provide data on global statistics and indicators through a simple API.

How to do it...

We use jQuery's `getJSON` function to query The World Bank's Cellular Indicator API and manipulate the data before displaying pie charts with Flot:

```
var getDataPage = function (url, cb, page, data) {
  return function (response) {
    var newData = response[1];
    newData.unshift(newData.length);
    newData.unshift(data.length);

    // append new data to existing data
    data.splice.apply(data, newData);

    // get more data if there are more pages
    if (response[0].pages > page) {
      getData(url, cb, page + 1, data);
    }
    else {
      cb(data);
    }
  };
};

var getData = function (url, cb, page, data) {
  page = page || 1;
  data = data || [];

  $.getJSON(
    url + '&page=' + page,
    getDataPage(url, cb, page, data)
  );
};

var excludeInvalidData = function (d) {
    // Some data has a null value or actually
    // represents groups of countries.
    return (
      d.value &&
      !/\d/.test(d.country.id) &&
      !/^x/i.test(d.country.id) &&
      ['OE', 'ZJ', 'ZQ', 'ZG', 'ZF', 'EU'].
        indexOf(d.country.id) === -1
    );
};
```

```javascript
var makeFormatter = function (power, suffix) {
  return function (label, series) {
    return (
      label + '<br />' +
      (
        series.data[0][1] / Math.pow(10, power)
      ).toFixed(0) + ' ' +
      suffix
    );
  };
};

var options = {
  series: {
    pie: {
      show: true,
      label: {
        show: true,
        formatter: makeFormatter(6, 'M')
      }
    }
  }
};

var plotData = function (rawData) {
  var data = rawData.
    filter(excludeInvalidData).
    map(function (d) {
      return {
        label: d.country.value,
        data: parseFloat(d.value)
      };
    });

  data.sort(function (a, b) { return b.data - a.data; });

  var topFive = data.slice(0, 5);
  $('#topFive').plot( topFive, options );

  var bottomFive = data.slice(-5);
  options.series.pie.label.formatter =
    makeFormatter(3, 'K');
  $('#bottomFive').plot( bottomFive, options );
};

getData(
  'http://api.worldbank.org/' +
  'countries/all/indicators/IT.CEL.SETS/?' +
  'format=jsonp&prefix=?&date=2011:2011',
  plotData
);
```

The resulting pie charts depict the number of cellular subscription for the top five and bottom five countries in the world:

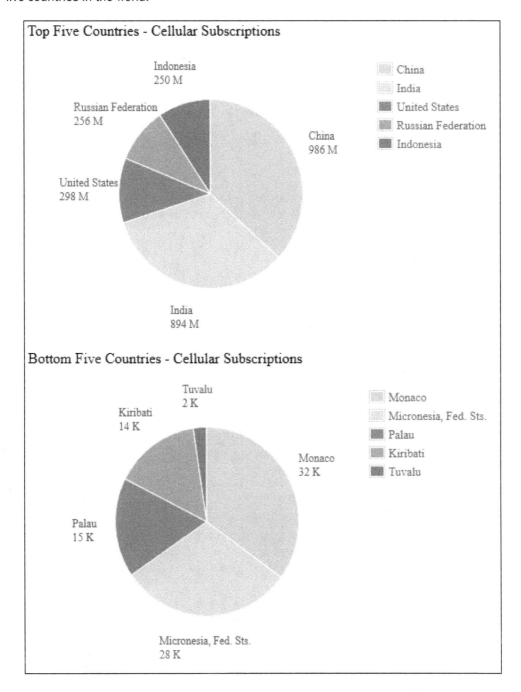

How it works...

The API returns a JSON structure that includes several pieces of information, but we are really only interested in the country name and the number of cellular subscriptions. We first filter out some invalid data with JavaScript's `filter` function, and then map the relevant values to the format that Flot expects for pie charts.

We sort the data, and then extract the top and bottom five countries. Finally, we display pie charts for the data sets with a custom pie label formatter that shows the number of subscriptions in millions or thousands.

There's more...

The following example shows some personal data analysis. We take weight loss data collected over several years and analyze it using custom averaging and trend calculations:

```
. . .
<script>
  var weightData;
  var goalWeight = 70;
  var MS_PER_DAY = 24 * 60 * 60 * 1000;

  var parseDate = function (d) {
    // Turn a string like '2013-08-18'
    // into a timestamp.
    var dateParts = d[0].split('-');
    var timestamp = new Date(
      parseInt(dateParts[0], 10),
      parseInt(dateParts[1], 10) - 1,
      parseInt(dateParts[2], 10)
    ).getTime()
    return [ timestamp, d[1] ];
  };

  var calculateRunningAvg = function (data, i, arr) {
    // return a data point which has a y-value
    // that is the average of the previous 10 y-values
    // in the array.
    var pointsToAverage =
      arr.slice(Math.max(0, i - 9), i + 1);
    var sum = pointsToAverage.reduce(function (a, b) {
        return a + b[1];
    }, 0);
```

```
    var average =  sum / Math.min(i + 1, 10);
    return [ data[0], average ];
};

var calculateSlope = function (p1, p2) {
  var rise = p2[1] - p1[1]
  var run = p2[0] - p1[0];
  return rise / run;
};

var calculateTrend = function (arr) {
  var n = arr.length - 1;
  var slope = calculateSlope(arr[n - 1], arr[n]);
  var trend = [];
  var start = arr[n];

  // If the slope is positive or close to 0,
  // calculate a trend 10 days in to the future.
  // Otherwise, calculate the trend until it
  // meets the goal weight.
  for (
    var i = 0, y = start[1];
    slope >= -1e-10 ? i < 10 : y > goalWeight;
    i++
  ) {
    var x = start[0] + i * MS_PER_DAY;
    y = start[1] + i * MS_PER_DAY * slope;
    trend.push([x, y]);
  }
  return trend;
};

var filterToPeriod = function (data, period) {
  if (period) {
    var start = data[data.length - 1][0] - period;
    data = data.filter(function (d) {
      return d[0] > start;
    });
  }
  return data;
};
```

```
    var plotWeight = function (rawData, period) {
      weightData = weightData || rawData;

      var data = rawData.map(parseDate);

      data = filterToPeriod(data, period);

      var runningAverage = data.map(calculateRunningAvg);

      var trend = calculateTrend(runningAverage);

      var goalWeightLine = [
        [data[0][0], goalWeight],
        [trend[trend.length - 1][0], goalWeight]
      ];

      $('#weight').plot(
        [
          data,
          { label: 'Average', data: runningAverage },
          { label: 'Trend', data: trend },
          { label: 'Goal weight', data: goalWeightLine },
        ],
        {
          xaxis: { mode: 'time' },
          legend: { show: true, position: 'sw' }
        }
      );
    };

$('#oneYear').click(function () {
  plotWeight(weightData, 12 * 30 * MS_PER_DAY);
});
$('#threeMonths').click(function () {
  plotWeight(weightData, 3 * 30 * MS_PER_DAY);
});
$('#oneMonth').click(function () {
  plotWeight(weightData, 30 * MS_PER_DAY);
});
$('#all').click(function () {
  plotWeight(weightData, null);
});

plotWeight([
  ['2010-01-20',97.25],
  ['2010-01-21',96.98],
  ['2010-01-22',97.25],
  ...
  ['2013-08-29',77.30],
```

```
        ['2013-08-30',75.00],
        ['2013-09-02',74.60]
    ]);

    </script>
...
```

The resulting chart shows the raw weight data with an overlaid running average, a trend line and a goal line. The code also adds interactivity to the chart via buttons that dynamically change the visible date range; effectively allowing the user to zoom in on the data.

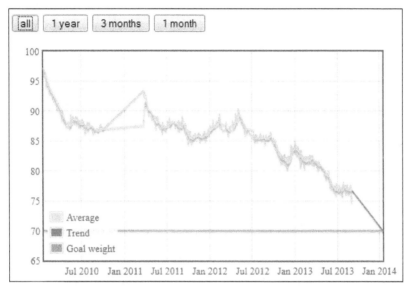

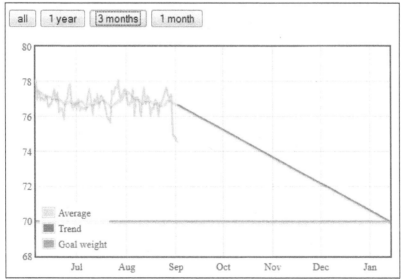

Creating custom plugins (Become an expert)

As we've seen so far, many of Flot's capabilities come from plugins. Flot's extensibility is one of its best features. It allows us to add custom functionality easily and organizes our code into manageable modules.

How to do it...

Here, we extract the running average functionality that we built in the *There's more...* section and put it into a custom plugin. This allows us to display the running average of any dataset with a simple setting:

```
. . .
  <script>
    (function ($) {
      var calculateRunningAverage=function (data, numPoints) {
        return data.map(function (point, i, arr) {
          var pointsToAverage =
            arr.slice(Math.max(0, i - numPoints + 1), i + 1);
          var sum = pointsToAverage.reduce(function (a, b) {
            return a + b[1];
          }, 0);
          var average =  sum / Math.min(i + 1, numPoints);
          return [ point[0], average ];
        });
      };

      var addRunningAverage = function (plot, series) {
        if (
          series.runningAverage &&
          series.runningAverage.show
        ) {
          var allData = plot.getData();

          var averageData = calculateRunningAverage(
            series.data, series.runningAverage.numPoints);

          allData.push({
            data: averageData,
            color: series.runningAverage.color
          });
```

```
      // disable the hook to prevent infinite recursion.
      plot.hooks.processRawData =
        plot.hooks.processRawData.filter(function (x) {
          return x !== addRunningAverage;
        });

      plot.setData(allData);

      plot.hooks.processRawData.push(addRunningAverage);
    }
  };
  var init = function (plot) {
    plot.hooks.processRawData.push(addRunningAverage);
  };
  var options = {
    series: {
      runningAverage: {
        show: false,
        numPoints: 2,
        color: 'red'
      }
    }
  };
  $.plot.plugins.push({
    name: 'runningAverage',
    version: '0.1.0',
    init: init,
    options: options
  });
}(jQuery));

var data = [
  [0, 240], [1, 228], [2, 312], [3, 272], [4, 335],
  [5, 348], [6, 348], [7, 320], [8, 351], [9, 341],
  [10, 336], [11, 343], [12, 410], [13, 372], [14, 369],
  [15, 425], [16, 375], [17, 377], [18, 479], [19, 439]
];
var data2 = data.map(function (d) {
  return [d[0], d[1] + 200];
});
var dataset = [
  { data: data, runningAverage: {show: true} },
```

```
        { data: data2, runningAverage: {
          show: true, numPoints: 8
        } }
    ];

    $.plot(
      $('#sample'),
      dataset,
      { lines: { show: true } }
    );
  </script>
...
```

We use our plugin to display the running averages (in red) of two series, but with different intervals for the average:

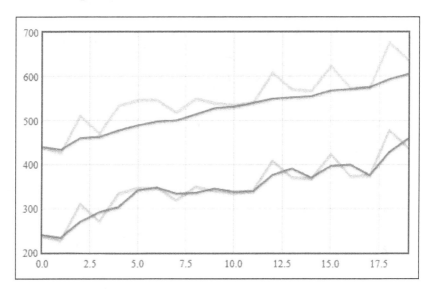

How it works...

We start our plugin by containing it inside a closure. This allows us to code our plugin without having to worry about contaminating the global scope. We pass the jQuery object into the closure so that we can access and extend Flot with our plugin:

```
(function ($) {
...
} (jQuery);
```

Next, we define our plugin. It consists of three functions; `calculateRunningAverage`, `addRunningAverage`, and `init`; and one `options` object. The `init` function is the starting point of our plugin. Our plugin hooks into Flot's rendering pipeline at the `processRawData` phase, which occurs just before Flot interprets the data passed to it. We add our `addRunningAverage` function to the hook array. The function will be called once for every series in the dataset being plotted.

The `addRunningAverage` function uses the plot's `getData` and `setData` methods to retrieve the dataset and add the new running average data for the current series. Note that we must remove our hook before we call `setData` because `setData` calls `processRawData` internally, causing an infinite recursion. We then add the hook back after `setData` has been called.

Finally, we make Flot aware of our plugin by adding a plugin object to the `$.plot.plugins` array. The plugin object gives Flot some metadata about our plugin and tells it about our plugin's starting point, the `init` function. The object also includes the default options for our plugin. By convention, the options are set to disable the plugin by default; in this case, the `show` setting is set to `false` so that users of the plugin can choose to opt in to the plugin as they please.

Flot merges the default options with its options and the options on the individual series when a plot is made.

There's more...

Our example plugin is very simple, but Flot's powerful extensibility allows plugins to do all sorts of things. For example, you could hook into Flot's rendering phases and draw arbitrary graphics directly onto the canvas, or you could bind to mouse and keyboard events on a plot to respond to user interaction.

You can learn more about plugins in the following Flot's documentation:

- **Hooks**: `https://github.com/flot/flot/blob/0.8.1/API.md#hooks`
- **Introduction to plugins**:
  `https://github.com/flot/flot/blob/0.8.1/API.md#plugins`
- **More plugin information**:
  `https://github.com/flot/flot/blob/0.8.1/PLUGINS.md`

HTML5 Data and Services Cookbook

ISBN: 978-1-783559-28-2   Paperback: 480 pages

Over one hundred website building recipes utilizing all the modern HTML5 features and techniques!

1. Learn to effectively display lists and tables, draw charts, animate elements and use modern techniques such as templates and data-binding frameworks through simple and short examples.

2. Examples utilizing modern HTML5 features such as rich text editing, file manipulation, graphics drawing capabilities, real time communication.

3. Explore the full power of HTML5 - from number rounding to advanced graphics to real-time data binding - we have it covered.

Matplotlib for Python Developers

ISBN: 978-1-847197-90-0   Paperback: 308 pages

Build remarkable publication-quality plots the easy way

1. Create high quality 2D plots by using Matplotlib productively

2. Incremental introduction to Matplotlib, from the ground up to advanced levels

3. Embed Matplotlib in GTK+, Qt, and wxWidgets applications as well as web sites to utilize them in Python applications

Please check **www.PacktPub.com** for information on our titles